AF269746

Fast Fighter Jets

Brianna Kaiser

Lerner Publications ◆ Minneapolis

Lerner Publications Company
An imprint of Lerner Publishing Group, Inc.
241 First Avenue North
Minneapolis, MN 55401 USA

For reading levels and more information, look up this title at www.lernerbooks.com.

Main body text set in Billy Infant Regular. Typeface provided by SparkType.

Editor: Nicole Berglund **Photo Editor:** Nicole Berglund

Library of Congress Cataloging-in-Publication Data

Names: Kaiser, Brianna, 1996- author.
Title: Fast fighter jets / Brianna Kaiser.
Description: Minneapolis : Lerner Publications, [2025] | Series: Lightning bolt books ® - Mighty military vehicles | Includes bibliographical references and index. | Audience: Ages 6-9 | Audience: Grades 2-3 | Summary: "How does the air force battle enemies in the sky? They use fighter jets. Readers will enjoy exploring the ins and outs of fighter jets to understand the technology that makes these aircraft work"— Provided by publisher.
Identifiers: LCCN 2023036354 (print) | LCCN 2023036355 (ebook) | ISBN 9798765626115 (library binding) | ISBN 9798765628959 (paperback) | ISBN 9798765635124 (epub)
Subjects: LCSH: Jet fighter planes—Juvenile literature.
Classification: LCC UG1242.F5 K35 2025 (print) | LCC UG1242.F5 (ebook) | DDC 623.74/64—dc23/eng/20230801

LC record available at https://lccn.loc.gov/2023036354
LC ebook record available at https://lccn.loc.gov/2023036355

Manufactured in the United States of America
1-1009903-51945-9/29/2023

Table of Contents

A Loud Boom

A fighter jet zooms past at over 1,000 miles (1,609 km) an hour. A loud boom echoes in the sky!

Fighter jets are fast aircraft made for the military. They create a loud boom because they fly so fast.

Militaries use jets to fight enemies in war. They also use them to control the sky over a battlefield.

Pilots control most fighter jets. They sit in a cockpit, a small space at the front. They steer the jet with a control stick.

Some fighter jets can fly without pilots. These jets have special computers to control them.

The X-62A is controlled by computers.

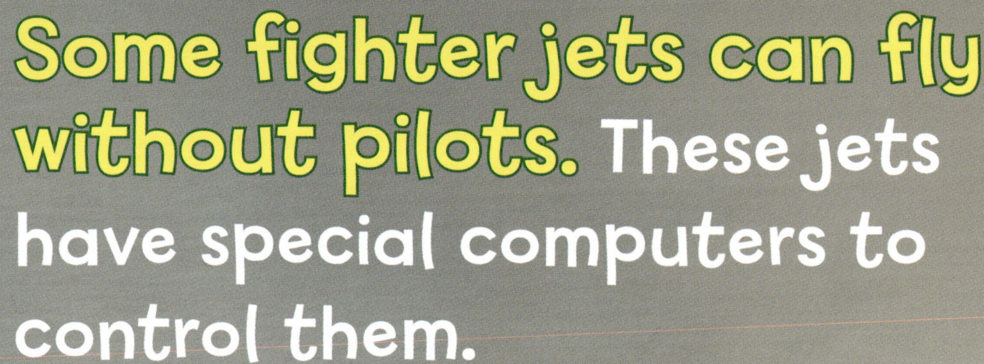

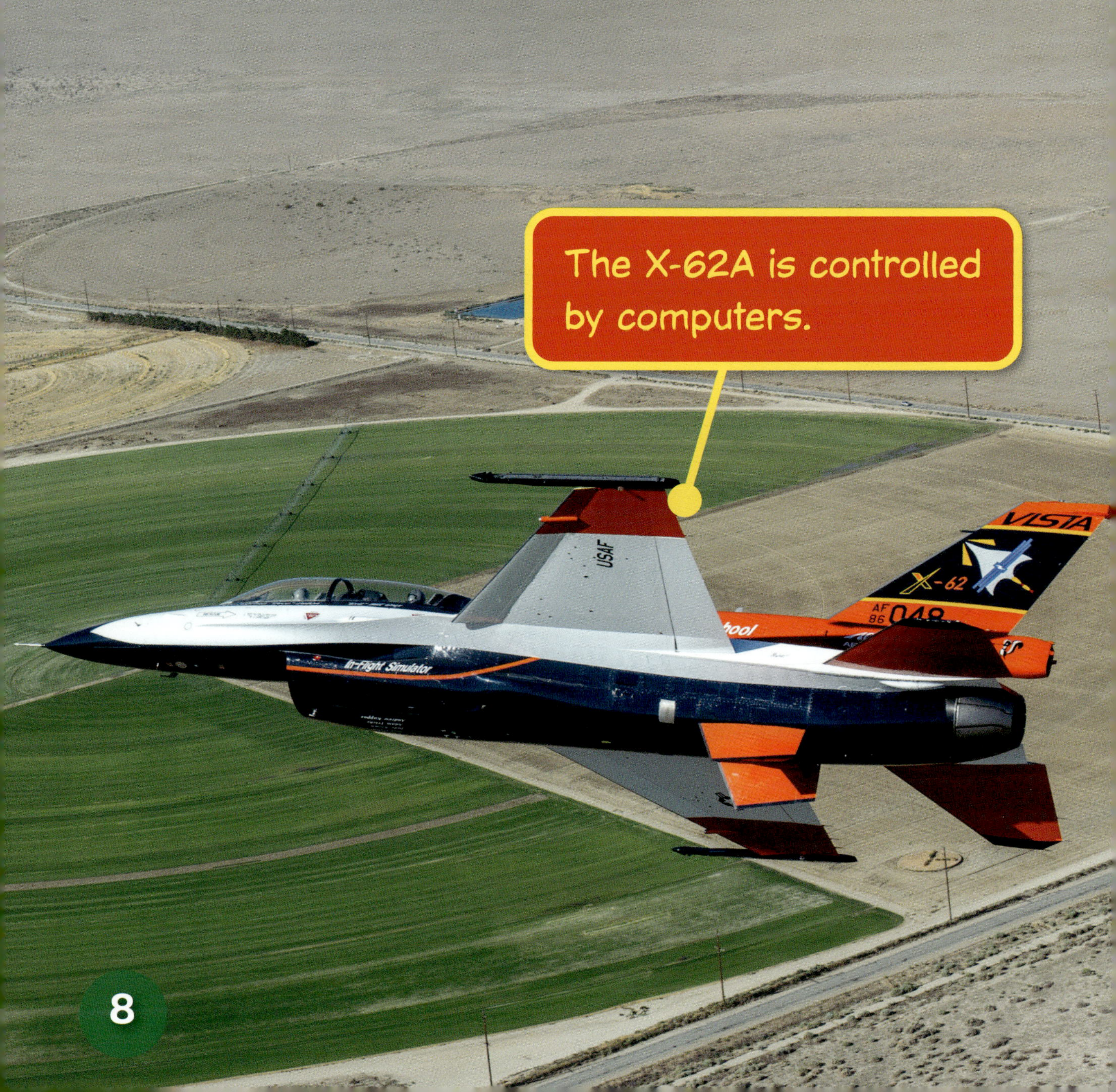

The throttle controls the flow of fuel.

Fighter jets have powerful engines. Pilots use a throttle to control the engine.

Cool Parts

Fighter jets have cool tech. They help pilots do tasks during their missions.

Radar tracks the location of
objects and other aircraft.
It helps pilots to not hit
anything.

Fighter jets have weapons such as missiles, bombs, and machine guns. Pilots may use these weapons to fight enemy jets.

Many fighter jets have stealth tech. This tech makes it harder for jets to be seen on the radar of other jets. Stealth tech helps them be sneaky.

Some fighter jets have one or two nozzles. They are at the back of the jet. They have flaps that point up or down to turn the jet.

Fighter jets can be light or heavy. Heavier fighter jets have stronger engines and more space for fuel. They can fly longer distances.

Many Missions

Militaries use fighter jets for many kinds of missions. The missions can have different goals.

Some fighter jets focus on combat. They find and fight enemy jets.

Other fighter jets focus on getting info to learn more about enemies. They may learn what kinds of weapons an enemy has.

Fighter jets are getting faster and better at completing missions. What tech do you think will be added to them next?

The US Navy Blue Angels perform a show with fighter jets.

Fighter Jet Diagram

F-35 Lightning II

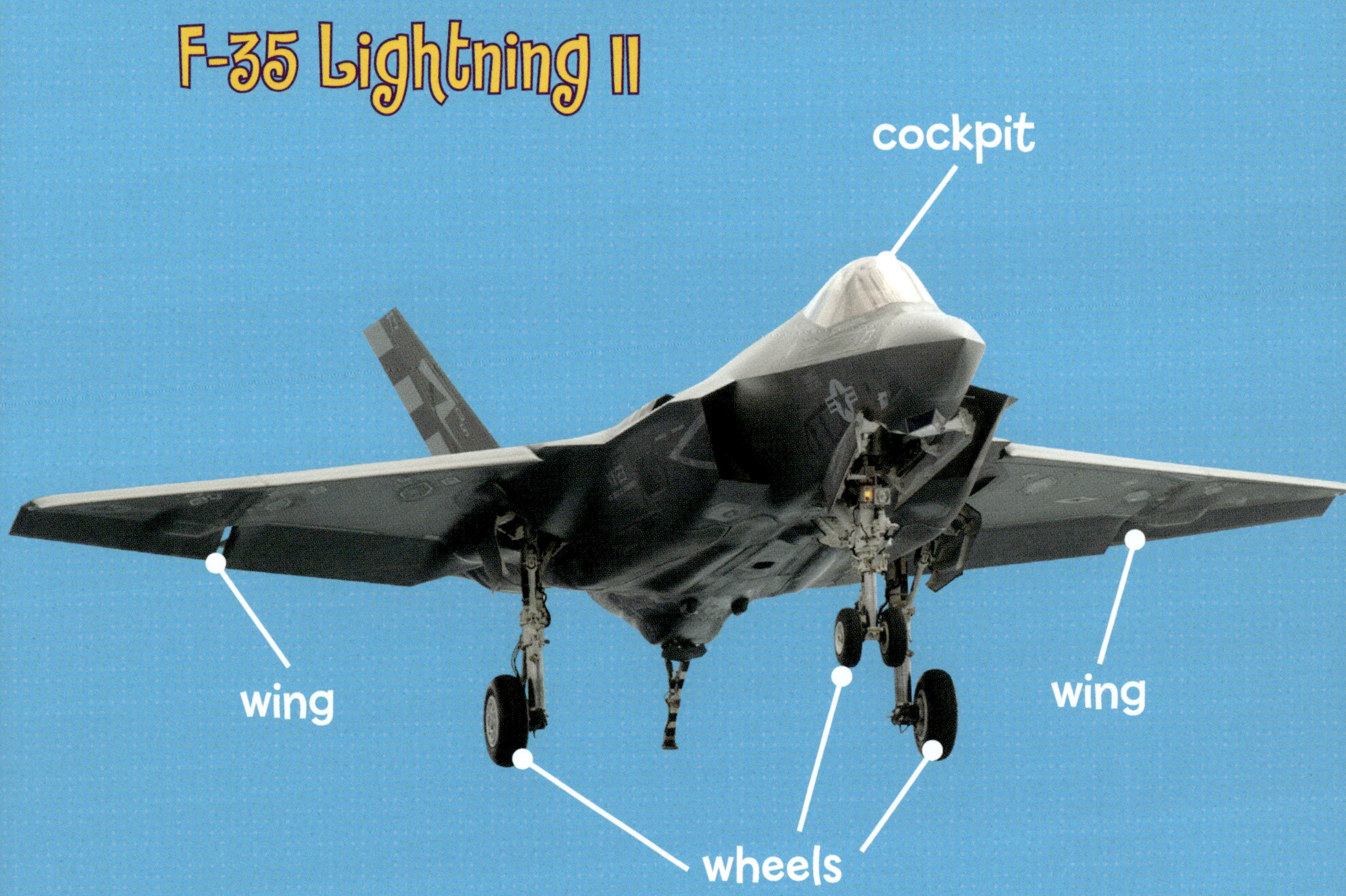

Fun Facts

- The fastest fighter jet in history, the X-15, flew at 4,520 miles (7,274 km) an hour.

- Fighter jets were slower during World War II (1939–1945). They flew at about 450 miles (724 km) an hour.

- Countries may work together to create fighter jets. China and Pakistan worked together to make the JF-17 Thunder.

Glossary

combat: a fight or battle

mission: an important task or goal a person or group works toward

nozzle: a part that controls the direction gas flows as it exits the jet

radar: tech that tracks the location of objects

stealth: tech that makes it harder to be seen

tech: short for *technology*, tools used to complete a task

throttle: a part of an engine that controls the flow of fuel

Learn More

Britannica Kids: Air Force
https://kids.britannica.com/kids/article/air-force
/352717

Ducksters: World War II Aircraft
https://www.ducksters.com/history/world_war_ii
/ww2_aircraft.php

Henzel, Cynthia Kennedy. *Powerful Military Aircraft*.
Parker, CO: Child's World, 2023.

Kiddle: Fighter Aircraft Facts for Kids
https://kids.kiddle.co/Fighter_aircraft

Miller, Marie-Therese. *Speedy Drones*. Minneapolis:
Lerner Publications, 2025.

Ransom, Candice. *How Fighter Jets Work*.
Minneapolis: Lerner Publications, 2020.

Index

Photo Acknowledgments

Image credits: U.S. Navy photo by Danette Baso Silvers, p. 4; U.S. Air Force photo by Airman 1st Class Andrew D. Sarver, p. 5; U.S. Air Force photo by 1st Lt Savanah Bray, p. 6; U.S. Air Force photo by Tech. Sgt. Erik Cardenas, p. 7; U.S. Air Force photo by Kyle Brasier, p. 8; U.S. Air Force photo by Airman First Class Zachary Rufus, p. 9; U.S. Air National Guard photo by Audra Flanagan, p. 10; U.S. Air Force photo by Airman 1st Class James Kennedy, p. 11; Air National Guard photo by Senior Master Sgt. Beth Holliker, p. 12; U.S. Air Force photo by Airman 1st Class Steven Cardo, p. 13; U.S. Air National Guard photo by Airman Basic Jakob Ivanick, p. 14; U.S. Air Force photo by Senior Airman Alexander Cook, p. 15; U.S. Air Force photo by Staff Sergeant Roslyn Ward, p. 16; U.S. Air National Guard photo by Senior Master Sgt. Andrew J. Moseley, p. 17; South Carolina Air National Guard photo by Senior Master Sgt. Edward Snyder, p. 18; U.S. Navy photo by Eric Parsons, p. 19; U.S. Navy photo courtesy Lockheed Martin by Andrew McMurtrie, p. 20.

Cover: U.S. Air Force photo by Staff Sgt. Sergio A. Gamboa.